YOUR KNOWLEDGE HAS VALUE

- We will publish your bachelor's and master's thesis, essays and papers

- Your own eBook and book - sold worldwide in all relevant shops

- Earn money with each sale

Upload your text at www.GRIN.com
and publish for free

Presence, history and expected future development of BenQ

Daniela Margardt

Bibliographic information published by the German National Library:

The German National Library lists this publication in the National Bibliography; detailed bibliographic data are available on the Internet at http://dnb.dnb.de.

ISBN: 9783668331020
This book is also available as an ebook.

© GRIN Publishing GmbH
Trappentreustraße 1
80339 München

Print and binding: Books on Demand GmbH, Norderstedt, Germany
Printed on acid-free paper from responsible sources.

The present work has been carefully prepared. Nevertheless, authors and publishers do not incur liability for the correctness of information, notes, links and advice as well as any printing errors.

GRIN web shop: https://www.grin.com/document/127370

Hochschule für Technik und Wirtschaft des Saarlandes

FACHBEREICH BETRIEBSWIRTSCHAFT

STUDIENGANG: International Management, Master

1. Semester

HAUSARBEIT

THEMA: Presence, history and expected future development of the Taiwanese Company
BENQ

NAME: Daniela Margardt

Abgabe: 16.02.2007

List of Abreviations and Acronyms

AG	Aktiengesellschaft
BDH	Bosch-Siemens-Hausgeräte
BenQ	Bringing Enjoyment and Quality to Life
BOT	Built, Operate, Transfer
CEO	Chief Executive Officer
CIS	CIS countries: Armenia, Moldova, Belarus, Kyrghyzstan, Tajikistan, Turkmenistan, Uzbekistan, Kazakhstan, Ukraine, Azerbajan and Georgia
Corp.	Corporation
DRAM	Dynamic Random Access Memory
etc.	et cetera
GSM	Global System for Mobile Communications
IG-Metall	Industriegewerkschaft Metall
IMS	IP (Internet) based Multimedia Subsystem
Inc.	Incorporated
IT	Information Technology
LC	liquid crystal
LG	LG Electronics Inc.
LCD	liquid crystal display
Ltd.	Limited
mio.	million
R&D	Research and Development
SF	San Francisco
TFT	thin film transistor
TV	Television

Table of Content

1. Introduction

1.1 Presentation of the problem

The mobile phone market has increased significantly worldwide over the last years. Mobile communication is becoming more relevant due to the rising importance of all time mobility, flexibility, reachability and information. There is a future tendency for the exclusive use of mobile phones. The mobile phone is a status symbol and it is easier and cheaper to communicate through them than through telephone mainlines in terms of mainline implementation costs. Implementation costs for mainlines are considerably higher. Mobile phones offer many additional functions such as text messaging, phone book, contacts, remember functions, Internet access, bluetooth, TV and much more. In 2006 the worldwide sales of mobile phones increased by 25% compared to 2005. Approximately 1 billion mobile phones had been sold. The main reason is emerging markets with much lower teledensity and the replacement of older mobile phones with new ones. In 2006 Nokia had been the worldwide market leader with 34,1% (2005:~33%) of the market shares followed by Motorola (21,3%), Samsung (11,6%), Sony Ericsson (7,3),LG (6,3%) and others.[1] Nokia had a turnover of 19% that means 24.8 billion Euro. This Finnish company is the largest mobile phone producer in the world. One reason for the growth of Nokia in 2006 had been the situation of BenQ Siemens. Their market shares could be distributed among all other market participants.

In the following years, the worldwide market growth rates will not grow significantly because consumers have to be perceived to adjust their mobile phones to latest trends. A decrease of 5% is expected. Causes are the market saturation, long-time contracts and no innovations.[2] In Germany, there is an expected increase of 3%, while turnover remains static.[3] However, over the last few years, the German mobile market was also marked by a constant growth. Actually, Germany's 82 mio. inhabitants own more than 82.2 mio. mobile phones. Statistically, every infant as well as every elderly person possess a mobile phone. In reality, some people do not have a mobile phone while others own two or three. The turnover for cell phones had been 3.9 billion Euro in 2006. Companies mainly compete on prices in the mobile phone market. Therefore the mobile phone sales increased by 2% in 2006 compared to 2005 while the turnover stays

---

[1] http://www.espace.ch/artikel_311424.html, 11.02.07
[2] http://www.inside-handy.de/news/6959.html, 10.01.07
[3] http://www.pressetext.at/pte.mc?pte=060929036, 10.01.07

5

constant.[4] That means that approximately 32 million mobile phones had been sold in 2006. In 2005 the growth rate in the mobile market had been 10% and 17% in 2004.

According to current news releases, there can be spoken about market saturation in the mobile phone market. But the German market is one of the European markets that is not that as saturated as others.[5] In the last years, the German cell phone market had been widely discussed in the news. Reasons for this have been the problems of the last German mobile phone producer Siemens with its mobile phone division and then finally the acquisition by BenQ. In the news, there is often the question of why did BenQ buy the mobile phone production from Siemens? Could one of the reasons be the potential of the German market? Since the announcement of the BenQ mobile phone division in Germany declaring bankruptcy, it is obvious that the German mobile phone production is at its end.

1.2 Structure of the thesis

In that thesis the current BenQ Siemens situation will be expatiated. First, there will be information about the Taiwanese company BenQ. This includes information on company itself as well as some highlights of its history which will be presented in order to provide an insight into the basics of BenQ. Furthermore, the current developments concerning the acquisition of the Siemens mobile phone division will be reflected. Afterwards, the market entry strategy of BenQ is observed in order to reveal the strategic reasons. Secondly, the Siemens company will be examined. The company's past will be reflected upon and the present situation is discussed within BenQ´s present developments because of the linkage of both firms through the mobile phone division. Some thoughts about the future of the BenQ Siemens mobile phone division are made. In the end, the conclusion will contain some personal thoughts about the approach of BenQ just as about the acting of Siemens. Finally, there is to say that this thesis has been an ongoing work over a certain time period. Therefore definitions about expressions as past, current and future are made at that point. In that thesis, past means historical events, present means occurrences within year 2005/ 2006 and the future is defined as events in the year 2007 and afterwards to include the latest available information. The basis of that thesis is information from newspapers, professional journals, TV news and the Internet.

---

[4] http://www.bitkom.org/de/presse/43408_41678.aspx, 19.01.07
[5] http://www.dw-world.de/dw/article/0,2144,2137023,00.html, 10.01.07

2. BENQ

2.1 Company Presentation

The BenQ Group was founded on April 21, 1984, and is an IT company acting worldwide. The headquarters are located in Gueishan, Taiwan. The multinational Group employs 18 000 employees[6] in more than 70 countries. In 2005 the main sales areas had been in the Americas (35%), Europe (28%), Asia, Pacific, Africa, Middle East (together 19%) and China (18%). The Taiwanese BenQ tries to operate according to its name, which stands for the vision **Bringing Enjoyment and Quality to Life** (BenQ). The Chairman is Kuen-yao Lee and the president is Sheaffer Lee. Both of whom are Taiwanese business man. The BenQ Group consists of 11 companies that work independent but share resources and profit from synergy effects. The different companies are " (...) AU Optronics Corporation, (...) Darfon Electronics Corporation; Daxon Technology Inc; Wellpower Optronics Co., Ltd.; Raydium Semiconductor Corporation; Airoha Technology Corporation; Cando Corporation; Darwin Precisions Co., Ltd,; BenQ Corporation; BenQ Hospital and BenQ Guru Software Co., Ltd. "[7] In 2005, BenQ´s revenue was US$ 12,36 billion dollars.[8]

2.1.1 Products and Services

BenQ classifies its products in three main categories. First: Computing, second: Consumer Electronics and third: Communications. Computing means the selling of products that are linked to the personal computer such as TV- sets, joybooks, keyboards, storage and monitors. But, computing suppose also the search for improvements and innovations such as recently launched LCD or Plasma monitors. The second sphere is the Consumer Electronics which is linked mostly to entertainment. These are products like cameras, projectors and displays. The third category is defined as Communications, meaning mobile phones. Today mobile phones cover various functions like communication, data transfer, music, cameras etc. BenQ tries to facilitate and improve human lifestyle through their products and services. Additionally, BenQ focuses on technology to maintain its position on the market in future. Technology includes Human Technology, Design Technology and Technology for Enjoyment.

[6] http://www.benq.com/page/?pageId=2, 24.11.06
[7] http://www.benq.com/page/?pageId=3, 25.10.06
[8] http://www.benq.com/page/?pageId=5, 12.11.06

BenQ owned following market shares in 2005: for 24% scanner, 14% projectors, 12% storage, 9,5% storage products and for 5% mobile phones.[9]

In 2006 BenQ produced as a third of its turnover mobile phones, next to notebooks, LC-screens, flatscreens and digital cameras.[10] In the past, BenQ produced especially in charge of other companies.

2.2 Company history

2.2.1 Past

According to the short general presentation of BenQ, I will go into details of BenQ´s history. BenQ´s history is also essential for the presence today and in future. First, I will begin with the past. Initially BenQ comes out of Acer Peripherals Inc., which was founded in 1984. In 1991, the name was changed into Acer Communications & Multimedia, probably due to marketing reasons and customer presence. Since 1996, the company expanded. In 1996, Acer Display Technologies Inc. and Darly Venture Inc. was established. In the next year, Darfon Electronics Corp. was built. Sales and marketing offices are located in Europe, America and Korea when the production facilities are in Taiwan (Tainan) and China (Suzhou). Darfon Electronics Corp. employees almost 14,000 people. Darfon develops and produces telecommunication components. The company acts worldwide and is viewed as the second largest supplier of keyboards for laptops and as the second largest supplier of LCD TV inverters. The company is growing due to the revenue 2004, 186 million US $, and 2005, 317 million US $. In 1998, Daxon Technology Inc. was founded. The company is the fifth largest manufacturer worldwide and is focused on thin-film technology products. The Daxon Technology Inc.´s headquarters is in Taiwan (Taoyuan) and the manufacturing locations were in Taiwan (Taoyuan), Malaysia (Penang) and in China (Suzhou). Daxon employs 2,384 employees and is growing comparing the revenue in 2004, 132,5 billion US $, to the revenue in 2005, 157 billion US $. The name BenQ appears the first time in 1998. BenQ Guru (Guru Systems) with headquarters and marketing and sales offices in Asia is established. BenQ Guru employs 350 employees and is an e-business solutions provider, such as supply chain management and human resources management. Finally in 2001, the BenQ company, with BenQ as the brand, is built. Headquarters is still in Taiwan, more exactly in Taoyuan and Taipei. For the first time in history, the company is not only oriented to

---

[9] http://benq.com/page/?pageId=5, 04.01.2007
[10] http://www.manager-magazin.de/magazin/artikel/0,2828,bild-691696-427713,00.html, 05.01.07

8

Asia, but also to Europe and America. The sales and marketing offices are in Europe, America, Asia Pacific and China. The year 2001 brings other important events. AU Optronics comes out of the merger of Acer Display Technologies Inc. and Unipac Optoelectronics Corp. Additional Airoha Technology Corp. is established. Airoha Technology Corp. employs 90 employees and is specialised on wireless technology and products. AU Optronics headquarters, R&D Center and manufacturing operations are in Asia. The sales and marketing offices are in Asia as well as in Europe and North America. In 2003 Philips and BenQ´s Digital Storage comes out of Royal Philips Electronics and BenQ. The headquarters is in Taiwan but Sales and Marketing are handled by the BenQ Corp. Cando Operations joins the BenQ Group in the same year. Cando includes 578 employees and is focused on manufacturing large-size colour filters. Further the BenQ hospital had been built in 2004. There are two hospitals, one in Nanjing and one in Suzhou. Both hospitals share the focus on incorporated services, a scope of 4,500 medical beds as well as equipment planning and management consultancy. In 2005, the most important event occured. BenQ bought Siemens mobile phone assembly division and relaunched the Siemens mobile phones under the name BenQ Siemens as a sub-brand. BenQ would increase its market shares in the mobile phone sector. The acquisition of the Siemens mobile phone division is the current problem of BenQ and further explained under the point BenQ´ history, Presence (chapter 2.2.2). In the last year, 2006, the focus had been on IT and optical storage products. To strengthen its position, especially to become the world´s best TFT and LCD supplier, AU Optronics, bought Quanta Display. The latest event had been the set up of BenQ´s IMS Business Group for comprising BenQ´s manufacturing operations. The headquarters is in Taiwan (Taoyuan) and the manufacturing sites are in different countries: Taiwan (Taoyuan), China (Suzhou), Mexico (Mexicali) and the Czech Republic (Brno).[11]

In sum, in BenQ´s past could be viewed, that the company is changing constantly. The BenQ Group is growing despite actual problems such as the difficulties with the BenQ Siemens cell phone division.

2.2.2 Present

The BenQ group has been present in the news, especially since the acquisition of the Siemens Mobile Phone division. To show the complexity of the actual BenQ Siemens discussion, it is essential to know about common basics of the two companies and the mobile phone assembly division.

---

[11] http://www.benq.com/page/?pageId=3, 11.12.06

9

In the beginning of 2005 Siemens announced that they had serious problems with the Mobile Phone division and that they were looking for a solution. In the first quarter of 2005, Siemens had a loss of 143 million Euro and significant sales slumps. BenQ announced the acquisition of the Siemens mobile phone division on 07.06.2005 including all gains and losses. The acquisition was on the first of October 2005. According to BenQ, Siemens had to buy BenQ shares for 50 million Euro and pay 250 million Euro for integration.[12] BenQ has the rights to use the co-brand Siemens during the next five years on mobile phones and for 18 months exclusive rights for the brand name Siemens. In return, the Taiwanese company has to ensure a long-run of the business, especially in Germany. In actual free press articles, it is published that Klaus Klein-feld, the CEO of Siemens, invested around 350 (400)[13] million Euro in the mobile phone division before selling.[14] BenQ invested around 800 million Euro in the German subsidiary. BenQ would amalgamate the Siemens mobile phone division with its own mobile phone division to increase gains and to profit from synergy effects. The partnership started in the beginning of the fourth quarter of 2005. The division employed 6000 employees. The intention of BenQ had been to become the fourth biggest mobile phone producer in the world and the biggest in Asia as a result of this acquisition. Siemens was willing to sell the division because the mobile phone division had been the loss-making division over the last few years. Christian Joos, the German BenQ-Mobile chief announced he was going to improve the mobile phone divisions quickly and to make profit through that division. Instead of increasing gains, BenQ also had problems with the mobile phone division. In July 2006, one year after the BenQ acquisition of the Sie-mens mobile phone division, BenQ announced to release employees. BenQ would like to eco-nomize 500 jobs in Germany. Jobs in the headquarters in Munich and external employees in Kamp-Lintford are concerned. The Taiwanese BenQ is looking for a solution. BenQ Mobile suffered from sales collapses and the loss of market shares. BenQ had serious problem with its German subsidiary from the beginning. For example: Mobile phones carried too late at sales points and the management had problems to be a unit. In the fourth quarter of 2006, BenQ achieved 51 million Euro in contrary to intended 391 million Euro.[15] BenQ's headquarters in Taipeh stopped to transfer money to its German subsidiary. In September 2006, the Taiwanese mobile phone producer BenQ announced its bankruptcy. 2000 of the 3000 employees looses

---

[12] http://www.benq.de/press/news.cfm?id=995&cat=0&year=2005, 10.12.06
[13] Saarbrücker Zeitung NR.2, Seite A6, 04.01.07
[14] http://www.stern.de/wirtschaft/unternehmen/unternehmen/572777.html?nv=ct_mt, 10.12.06
[15] http://de.today.reuters.com/news/newsArticle.aspx?type=topNews&storyID=2007-01-03T142012Z_01_KOE351599_RTRDEOC_0_DEUTSCHLAND-FIRMEN-BENQ-ZF.xml, 03.01.06

their jobs immediately. It could be seen that the Taiwanese company economize high redundancy payments through its bankruptcy. BenQ shut the german facilities but will use the trademark BenQ Siemens and patents from Asia. From the announcement of the insolvency, the company has to be out of losses. It is forbidden to be further in the red figures. BenQ was given a legal time limit to find an investor and to run the last pars of the business further on.

<u>2.2.3 Future</u>

In 2006 it was expected that BenQ will sell the mobile phone division to an unknown outsourcing specialist in 2007. BenQ is the last German mobile phone producer and it would be crucial if that industry division were to close. In October 2006, there are more than 100 companies that are interested to buy BenQ Mobile. There are negotiations with 31 of those companies and insider told that BenQ negotiated particularly with two big companies: Foxconn, a Taiwanese company and Jabil, an American company. It was expected that BenQ would sell the production facilities in Europe and China. Instead BenQ said all the time that they don´t want to sell. BenQ spoke from modifications because of the problems of BenQ Siemens mobile phones. The company was thinking about the closure of the production facility in Mexico and probably China.[16] To sell the mobile phone division would be the last possibility to save the BenQ Siemens mobile phone division and the belonging jobs. At the moment 3000 employees are concerned: 1600 in Kamp-Lintford and Bocholt and further 1400 employees in Munich. BenQ´s deadline to find an investor is at 31.12.2006 at 00:00. If BenQ cannot find an investor, the company will be closed and went into insolvency. The insolvency administrator Martin Prager said the possibility to find an investor is 50%. But the probability to find an investor until the end of 2006 is low. It would be better for an investor to buy in January 2007. Then the investor can takeover BenQ mobile without employees and brownfield like pension payments. That would be the only chance for the company, however bad for employees. The main problems to discuss are the rights to the brand name and patents. Until these two essential points are clarified, there will be problems to finding an investor. The insolvency administrator says that potential investors can receive information about these discussable points but other say that these two points are not clear enough. Another discussable point had been how much gains would be possible in future. On Friday morning, 28.12.05, one of the two investors jumped off of the negotiations due to its financial situation.[17] The last promise had been to find investors that will at least buy parts of

---

[16]http://www.spiegelgruppe.de/spiegelgruppe/home.nsf/pmweb/BB855CEFD0E80BB2C12571EF003___0AF28, 29.12.06

[17]http://www.wdr.de/themen/wirtschaft/wirtschaftsbranche/benq/061229.jhtml?rubrikenstyle=wirtsch

BenQ Mobile but it is doubtful if there could be found an investor who wants only to buy parts. But when investors buy parts they don't have to takeover commitments concerning employees. Best chances are expected for the BenQ subsidiary Inservio. It is known that there is an investor who will eventually busy the subsidiary and employ further 900 BenQ employees. But there is no concrete offer.[18]

On second January 2007, three month after the insolvency announcement, the insolvency administrator Martin Prager announced that he had not received a single offer from an investor. BenQ Mobile announced its final insolvency. The court of Munich opened the insolvency process on 03.01.2007. The insolvency administrator tries to make use of the BenQ mobile assets in the best way to satisfy the creditors. Theoretically, it is still possible to sell the BenQ Mobile division to an investor but not likely. 90% of employees went into a rescue company. That means that BenQ Mobile employs still 260 employees because of the end production until the end of January. End production means that all semi-finished mobile phones will be finished in the facility in Kamp-Lintford to sell them. 160 employees will work until the final closure.[19] According to latest press news in January, 400 employees found new jobs. 150 employees restart working at Siemens and the rest belongs now to so-called transfer companies in Bavaria and North Rhine-Westphalia, which are mostly financed by Siemens.

It is still possible to find an investor but it is more difficult to run the production the longer the production lines don't run.

2.3 Potential investors

BenQ Mobil is now looking for investors. In the beginning of 2007 there had been several companies that were interested in BenQ Mobil. Consecutively the most recent candidates are shown in order to explain their businesses and intentions.

---

aft, 02.01.06

[18]http://www.businessnews.com/business/art614,283628.html?fCMS=e523b5c6c9b9d1e9e11474abc1c95937, 03.01.07

[19]http://www.wdr.de/themen/kurzmeldungen/2007/01/01/hiobsbotschaft_fuer_benq-mitarbeiter.jhtml?rubrikenstyle=wirtschaft, 01.01.07; Saarbrücker Zeitung NR. 2, Seite A6, 04.12.06

2.3.1 Beha

Beha is a German American Investor group around the Daimler Chrysler IT manager Hans-Jörg Beha. Behind Beha are the SF Capital Partners, a private equity, with headquarters in California. Beha had the intention to employ 800 of the 3000 employees and to produce 4 mio. mobile phones in the high price segment in 2007. But Beha only would employ 800 employees under the condition that the employees will be paid by public authorities.[20] Hans-Jörg Beha claimed a 100 mio Euro bail from North Rhine-Westphalia but received a promise of only 20 mio. Euro.[21] The previous Daimler Chrysler manager pushed the insolvency administrator for a decision until 16th of January 2007 to start immediately with the production. Martin Prager indeed asked for a more detailed finance plan to understand how the purchase price and employees salaries will be paid. The German American investor group drew back their offer on Friday, the 19th of January 2007 because of the long procedure. Their concept could not be further realized.

2.3.2 Sentex SENSing

Sentex SENSing Technology inc. was founded in 1980. The president of the company is Henrik Rubinstein. The headquarters is based out of Cleveland, Ohio and the company employs 25 employees. The company's core business is in information technology equipment. They buy, sell and distribute computer equipment. The company planned to buy BenQ mobile to produce mobile phones with additional biometric functions within a high price segment. Sentex estimates that there will be a niche market for mobile phones with biometric functions. The mobile phones should have the functions to recognise fingermarks, face and voice recognition. The company will ensure 1800 to 2000 jobs[22] and they would like to start the production on 20th january 2007. Sentex offered 50 mio. Euro as purchase price but forced as security an Earn-Out model. That means that payments are paid dependant of the further business success. The company have no surplus and did not make any turnover during the last months.[23] In January 2007, the committee of inspection rejected the offer of Sentex.

---

[20] http://www.heise.de/newsticker/meldung/83269, 06.01.07

[21] http://www.heise.de/newsticker/meldung/83725, 19.01.2007

[22] http://www.faz.net/d/invest/meldung.aspx?id=39899560, 10.02.07;
http://www.sentextech.com/about.html, 10.02.07

[23] http://www.faz.net/d/invest/meldung.aspx?id=39897445, 19.01.2007; http://www.manager-magazin.de/it/artikel/0,2828,460342,00.html, 19.01.2007

2.3.3 Bacoc

Bacoc, the last potential investor for BenQ mobile announced to propose a concrete over on January 19th 2007 while working on a concrete finance plan. They did not meet that first deadline because their finance plan had not been finished. Bacoc is found in 1994 and their business is mobile computer systems and safety systems for mobile Office solutions. Bacocs headquarters is in Hamburg but the company has many branches in Great Britain, the United States and Spain. Their intention had been to close the headquarters in Munich and to keep the production facility in Kamp-Lintfort open. That would mean for the employees that 1000 jobs will be saved. Bacoc intended to produce 4,5 mio. mobile phones during 2007. On first February, the notebook producer announced not to invest.[24] One of the reasons for their withdrawal has been the decreasing chances for a restart. There are different causes for example that to many BenQ mobile employees from the production as well from the management left the company and the production is not full working since the announcement of the bankruptcy.

3. Siemens

3.1 Company presentation

The German company Siemens was founded by Werner von Siemens on the first of October 1847, in Berlin. The name had been Siemens & Halske. The name Halske was added for the mechanical engineer Georg Halske, who was responsible for construction. Siemens is one of the traditional companies in Germany and is an incorporated company. Ernst von Siemens had been the last chief executive from the Siemens family in 1968. The headquarters are located in Munich and Berlin. Since 2005 the CEO and chairman is Klaus Kleinfeld. Siemens and its subsidiaries are a worldwide operating company in more than 190 countries and employ 474,900 employees (in 2006).[25] Siemens is present in Africa, Middle East, CIS, the Americas, Asia, Australia and Europe.[26] Since the company's early developments, Siemens invested in other companies. Following, I will give a short overview about the three most important affiliates: Osram, Bosch-Siemens-Hausgeräte (BDH) and Fujitsu-Siemens. Osram has sales of 4,3 billion Euros, and is one of the leading lamp producers worldwide. Bosch-Siemens-Hausgeräte is a leading manufacturer of electrical consumer goods in Western Europe. In 1999, Fujitsu

---

[24] http://de.news.yahoo.com/070201/281/5b1ir.html, 02.02.07; http://en.bacoc.com/aboutus/aboutus.htm, 03.02.07; http://www.heise.de/newsticker/meldung/84675/from/rss09, 02.02.07

[25] http://www.siemens.com/index.jsp?sdc_p=ft4mls7uo1244571i1050364pcz2&sdc_bcpath=1327903.s_7,132895 4.s_7,1050364.s_7,&sdc_sid=426724783&, 18.11.06

[26] http://w4.siemens.de/archiv/en/laender.html, 04.12.06

Computers Ltd. and Siemens Division Computer Systems came together in a fusion and today the joint venture is the market leader in Germany as well as the European leading IT producer.[27] The sales in 2006 had been 87.325 billion Euro with a net income of 3.033 billion Euro.[28]

3.1.1 Products & Services

In almost each household there are products or available services from Siemens. Siemens is known for a variety of products which incorporate innovative technologies. The company gives its know- how to customers. Siemens speaks from products, solutions and services classified into business areas, industry and product name. The company classifies its products in different business areas such as: Automation and Control, Information and Communications, Medical, Power, Transportation and Service. Automation and Control cover Logistic Systems, Process Automation, Electrical Installation Technology etc. Information and Communications contains things such as Communication Services, Fixed and Mobile Networks, Information Technologies etc. The sector Medical envelop hearing solutions, refurbished systems, medical products and solutions etc. Power includes things like power supply, power transmission and distribution. Transportation deals with rail automation and electrification, turnkey systems for rail and integrated services for rail etc. The last business area is Service for example business, energy, financial or industrial services.[29] The next sector is industry containing healthcare like clinical segments; manufacturing industries for example mechanical engineering;, service industries like tourism and hotels; process and basic industries like cement, food and beverage and others; telecommunications for example network provider; transportation, logistics and infrastructure like airlines, rail traffic and marine traffic and others.[30] All in all Siemens owns more than 62 000 patents.

3.2 History

3.2.1 Past

Early years

---

[27]http://w4.siemens.de/archiv/en/beteiligungen/beteiligungen_akt.html, 18.11.06
[28]http://www.siemens.com/index.jsp?sdc_p=ft4mls7uo1244571i1050364pcz2&sdc_bcpath=1327903.s_7.132895
4.s_7.1050364.s_7.&sdc_sid=426724783&, 18.11.06

[29]http://www.siemens.com/index.jsp?sdc_p=fmls2uo1032974i1032974pcz3&sdc_bcpath=1327890.s_2.1032974.
s_2.&sdc_sid=430668491&, 18.11.06
[30]http://www.siemens.com/index.jsp?sdc_p=cfi11000000000015lmo1033036ps2uz3&sdc_bcpath=1327890.s_2
%2C1032974.s_2%2C&sdc_sid=430668491&sdc_m4r=, 18.11.06

As I gave some facts about BenQ's history, I will gave also some facts about Siemens history. Siemens is an old traditional German company and therefore the historical facts are wider explained than BenQ's.

In 1846, Werner von Siemens improved the Wheatstone Telegraph and designed so the new pointer telegraph. The mechanical engineer Georg Halske was responsible for the implementation. Both men founded their company Telegraphen-Bauanstalt von Siemens & Halske in 1847 in Berlin. In the same year, Werner von Siemens developed a gutta percha press. But the first big success was the order from the government to install a telegraph line between Berlin and Frankfurt/Main. From that point on, the company was constantly growing. Since the fifties, the company has been operating on an international level. In 1850, the company began operating on the British and later on the Russian market due to a crisis within Germany. In 1866, Werner von Siemens discovered the dynamo-electric principle. From that time, big quantities of electrical energy were possible. Electricity was spreading quickly. In 1879, the first electric railway was invented by Siemens & Halske according to the first electrical street lighting in Berlin. In 1880, the worldwide first electrical elevator was built in Mannheim and in Berlin were the worldwide first tramway in service. In 1890 Werner von Siemens retired and his brother Carl von Siemens and his sons Arnold and Willhelm led the company. In 1879, the company changed to a stock cooperation due to covering the companies growing capital requirements.[31]

Modifications

In 1903 the Siemens-Schuckertwerke GmbH was acquired to profit from synergy effects. In the next years, the company developed innovations like medical technic, wireless news transmission and in the twenties, after losses during the world war, white goods. The company lost 40 % of its capital during the war. In 1919, Carl Friedrich von Siemens became leader of the company and Osram GmbH and Co. KG (Osram comes from Osmium and Wolfram) is found of a joint venture of three companies including Siemens & Halske. In the twenties, the company belonged to the five leading companies working in light and heavy-current electrical engineering. During the next years, the company expanded. Some examples illustrating its growth are the foundation of the Japanese subsidiary Fusi Denki Seizo KK in 1923 as result of a joint venture of the Siemens-Schuckwerke GmbH and the Japanese Furukawa group. It was intended to produce in Japan. In 1924 the development of the Siemens D-Zug-radio, as well as the first

---

[31] http://w4.siemens.de/archiv/en/geschichte/zeitleiste/chronik_2.html, 18.11.06

16

traffic lights in Berlin. From 1923 to 1935, many plants were built. For example, a hydroelectronic power plant in Ireland in 1925, the Kraftwerk West in 1931 in Berlin or the Siemens Reiniger Werke in Erlangen in 1932. In 1928 the Siemens-Planiawerke AG and Vereinigte Eisenbahn-Signalwerke were developed etc. The next important event had been the invention of a Television Set by Telefunken. 50% of shares at Telefunken belonged to Siemens. In 1939 Siemens & Halske AG acquired all shares of Siemens-Schuckertwerke. In 1941, Carl Friedrich von Siemens death and Hermann von Siemens took over the company as chairman. During the second world war, the company was seriously damaged. In 1945, Ernst von Siemens was responsible for the Group Directorates outside Berlin.[32]

After second world war until 2007

During the second world war, the number of employees increased because of increased state demand and the production for the German army. Siemens employed as many other companies during that time forced labor. After the war, Siemens operated further within Germany and since internationally since the fifties. During the fifties, Siemens developed the floating zone method for production of ultra-pure silicon, started to work with data processing, founded the Siemens Elektrogeräte AG, developed the first electronical control system "Siemens 2002" and the first cardiac pacemaker which has been developed as well as produced at Siemens in Sweden. In the early sixties, the first electronically controlled telephone comission is built up in Munich. In upper Bavaria, the raisting Earth station is constructed. In the late sixties Siemens went on the stock market. Siemens founded the Bosch Siemens Hausgeräte GmbH, the Kraftform Union and the Transformatoren Union. These development let Siemens regain their position in the worldmarket market in the sixties. In 1966 the three main companies Siemens & Halske, Siemens- Schuckertwerke AG and Siemens-Reiniger-Werke AG merged to Siemens AG. In 1969, there had been six independant operating divisions. The organizational structure changed several times until the recent day.[33] In the seventies the most important milestones had been the start with the production of large-scale integrated circuits, the computer telegraph to examine skulls and the order about the production of nine generators for the largest hydro electric power station in the world, which is located in Brazil. In 1988, Siemens started with the mass production of DRAM chips. In 1990 the Siemens Nixdorf Informationssysteme AG is established and in 1997 Siemens launches its first GSM cellular phone with a coloured display.

---

[32] http://w4.siemens.de/archiv/en/geschichte/zeitleiste/chronik_2.html, 18.11.06
[33] http://w4.siemens.de/archiv/en/dokumente/company_history_long.pdf, 18.11.06;
http://w4.siemens.de/archiv/en/dokumente/company_history.pdf, 18.11.06

In the new century, the most important work of Siemens had been the Transrapid in Shanghai which first voyage had been on the new years evening 2002. The latest milestone, as published by Siemens, had been a computer tomograph that gives better pictures of the whole body than ever.

3.2.2 Present

Siemens announced in 2005 that they have serious problems with their mobile phone division. In the first quarter of 2005, Siemens had a loss of 143 million Euro and significant sales slumps. Siemens lost significantly of its worldwide market shares since 2003. Not to repeat the present situation (means the Siemens situation in 2005) cf. 2.2.2., as BenQ and Siemens are linked through their present situation.[34]

3.2.3 Future

Legal repercussions

According to the opening of the insolvency process, employees and critic search for responsible. The IG-Metall and the main part of previous employees accuse the Siemens Management. The previous Siemens employees accuse Siemens for giving inaccurate information about the BenQ changeover in 2005. According to the IG Metall, Siemens did not tell employees that BenQ could not ensure to maintain jobs and production facilities because BenQ is a company without own capital .[35] Previous employees without jobs claim compensation for damages from Siemens. Employees claim that the employer-employee relationship with Siemens continues. Employees claim also that BenQ and Siemens did not focus the rehabilitation of the mobile phone division, but to get rid of the German employees. Employees underlay their claims on the fact that the Siemens mobile phone division was split into a Management corporation, an asset corporation and into the BenQ Mobile corporation and Co. Partnership. The redundancy payments for BenQ top managers had been ensured in the Management Corporation (Management GmbH). Assets as well as know-how had been transferred to the asset corporation (Asset GmbH). Finally the German employees, which had been threatened by insolvency had been transferred into the BenQ Mobile corporation and Co. Partnership (BenQ Mobile GmbH &Co. OHG). It is assumed that the capital of BenQ Mobile had been 25.000 Euro which is not enough to ensure the employee wages of one day. Instead it is expected that BenQ transferred know-

---

[34] see http://www.siemens.com/press/de/pressemitteilungen/?press=/de/pr_cc/2005/06_jun/axx200_1273833.htm
[35] http://www.businessnews.com/business/art614,276873.html, 03.01.07

how for almost a billion out of Germany. [36] Siemens react immediately on the employees claims. All employees that expressed public disagreement to the takeover from Siemens to BenQ had to withdrawal their accusations. If not they could not be a member in the transfer company. But then all requirements against Siemens would be gone. Some employees are still claiming at the court, some gave up and went to one of the rescue companies.

New Claims

In the start phase of the year 2007, new claims emerged as well as the exact sum of debts that BenQ mobile accumulated. Altogether debts are expected on 883 mio. Euro[37] and assets are expected on 310 mio. Euro[38]. BenQ now requests further money from Siemens. Officially Siemens did not confirm that new claims had emerged. The BenQ insolvency administrator Martin Prager request an amount of 100 mio. Euro from the previous parent group. The sum is based on a survey from December 2006 which had been debtees purpose-built. The amount is only an expectation and could be adjusted downwards but will probably undergo an upwards adjustment. Because it is unknown if all debtees reported their situation – that they are debtees – or not yet. These 100 mio. Euro had been one rate of the 400 mio. Euro which Siemens was obliged to pay to BenQ as contribution to the acquisition. The 100 mio. Euro should originally be paid in the end of 2006 but BenQ agreed to Siemens that Siemens kept them back. On one hand, there is a discussion about 50 mio. Euro which Siemens did not pay to BenQ in order to save for the employees protection and indemnity bonds. All Siemens BenQ mobile phones had been distributed with an guaranty of two years and therefore indemnity bonds have to be built. On the other hand, there is a discussion about the other 50 mio. Euro.[39] Now, BenQ claims that Siemens did not indicate the real situation of the mobile division when BenQ took over the division. In contrast Siemens says that they indicated the financial situation in a correct way and that the division of assets had been higher than the companies debts.[40] These new claims could be seen as show for the public. BenQ claims money from Siemens to show that Siemens

[36] http://www.spiegel.de/wirtschaft/0,1518,439919,00.html, 11.11.06;
http://www.n24.de/wirtschaft_boerse/unternehmen/article.php?articleId=90565, 29.12.06
[37] http://www.golem.de/0702/50376.html, 07.02.07
[38] http://www20.wissen.de/wde/generator/wissen/services/nachrichten/ftd/TM/159233.html, 08.02.2007
[39] http://www.manager-magazin.de/unternehmen/artikel/0,2828,464746,00.html, 08.02.07;
http://www.silicon.de/enid/wirtschaft_und_politik/25284, 09.02.07
[40] http://www.wallstreet-online.de/nachrichten/nachricht/1994563.html, 06.01.07;
http://www20.wissen.de/wde/generator/wissen/services/nachrichten/ftd/TM/159233.html, 08.02.07

is responsible. In contrast, Siemens holds BenQ responsible for the bankruptcy because of bad financial management.[41]

4. Market Entry

But where can start points be made to look for responsibility? The market entry and the entering companies behavior can give some information. When companies would operate on other markets, they have to carefully plan their entrance into the market. It is almost impossible to enter the market without adequate preparation. Every company enters markets via appropriate market entry strategies. Market entry strategies are the result of Strategic Management.

4.1 Strategy

A market entry strategy is a long-term oriented plan which indicates how to enter a foreign market or to built up production facilities in the foreign country. All external threats and opportunities should be considered. This is especially needed for Asian companies because they often have serious problems entering foreign markets, especially European markets. Problems could be the brandname, the foreign language or the different behaviour and mentality. The biggest challenge is often a lack of understanding the foreign culture. All these problems could be defined as market entry barriers next to high competition, customer habits etc. There are different market entry strategies that companies can choose. Which strategy companies prefer depends always from the company and its individual situation. The most important entry strategies are: Exporting. Licensing, Franchising, Joint Ventures, Acquisitions, Green-Field Development, Production Sharing, Turnkey Operations, BOT Concept or Management Contracts. Joint Ventures is known as the most used entry option.[42] Later I will show the market entry of the Taiwanese company BenQ on the European market.

4.1.1 Acquisitions

Acquisition is one of various market entry options. It means that one company purchases another company that is already working in that business. Acquisition is a popular and quick way to get access to a foreign market. In some countries it is difficult to enter a market via acquisitions because of problems finding a candidate company to buy. There are often problems to receive information about candidates for an acquisition. In some countries, it is not possible to

---

[41] http://www20.wissen.de/wde/generator/wissen/services/nachrichten/ftd/TM/159233.html, 08.02.07
[42] Prof. Dr. rer. pol. Glowik, International Market Entry Strategies, 2005, p. 8; Wheelen/Hunger, Strategic Management and Business Policy, page 139

takeover a company due to restrictions about foreign ownerships. Growth Strategies are very common because of economies of scale effects, further market potentials like globalization and the pressure of global competition. Acquisition is an external growth strategy. In 2005, BenQ choosed Acquisitions as market entry strategy to strengthen its international position and grow horizontally to enter the Western and Eastern markets.

4.1.2 Acquisition BenQ Siemens

BenQ acquired the Siemens Mobile Phone division from Siemens. In contrary, Siemens bought BenQ shares for 50mio. Euro to participate. According to Siemens is BenQ from that point on seen as the preferred end-to-end partner. Further 'Siemens had to pay 250 mio. Euro for integration.

BenQ took over the production facilities in Manaus (Brazil) and Kamp-Lintford (Germany). Also, the management functions like the headquarters and the research and development functions were acquired by BenQ. The headquarters is in Munich.

BenQ chooses its market entry via the acquisition of the Siemens mobile phone division.

The BenQ strategy is explained by K. Y. Lee: "Our expansion strategy will be strongly supported by this deal, as we can rely on a global organization with excellent employees, a well-established blue-chip customer base in the mobile business and a strong brand with high impact. I welcome the addition of Siemens's management resources and look forward to working with the Siemens team on the combined platform. I am fully convinced that the acquisition provides many opportunities to strengthen our business in the consumer market and I am sure that our shareholders will share this opinion." [43]

4.2 Reasons

There could be various reasons for entry into a market. In the world of constant growing and globalization it is assumed that going international is related to a companies long-term business success. Reasons for an acquisition could be internally reasons, competition reasons or strategic reasons to get bigger. Further I will explain some reasons for BenQ to entry the market via the acquisition of the Siemens mobile phone division.

---

[43]http://www.siemens.com/index.jsp?sdc_p=cd1034230fi1273833lmn1031735o1273833ps5uz1&, 05.01.07

4.2.1 Management

On first place, BenQ could understand the European mentality, beliefs and values through the Siemens management. As a Taiwanese company, BenQ has definitely a lack of Western management. Through the acquisition, Siemens managers will become BenQ managers and so BenQ has access to Western management. Through the marriage of BenQ and Siemens, it was possible for BenQ to see how to deal with European or Latin American companies for example suppliers, distributors or retailers. BenQ could use the Siemens mobile phone division also to see how Siemens work in Latin America because of their experience.

4.2.2 Reputation

BenQ expected to create a new worldwide brand. The intention had been to become the fourth biggest mobile phone producer in the world and the biggest in Asia. With the acquisition of the Siemens mobile phone division, BenQ would conqueror the European and Latin American markets where Siemens is in a leader position in terms of reputation. BenQ is well known in Asia, but not very well in Western, Eastern Europe and Latin America. The Taiwan company would grow. Kuen-yao Lee, chairman of BenQ said that he would like that BenQ is known all over the world. For example like its competitors Philips or Sony. But the question is why did they choose Siemens? First, Siemens looked for an investor for its loss making mobile phone division and therefore it was easy for BenQ to buy the Siemens mobile phone division. But more important is the fact that Siemens is in Europe and Latin America recognised as a traditional brand to rely on. The union with a Western company would definitely increase the chances on the market for an Asian company by transferring the Siemens image on BenQ. Then the sales possibilities for other BenQ products would increase at the same time.

4.2.3 Access in detail

With the acquisition of the mobile phone division, BenQ gained access to customers, sales and distribution network especially on the European market. For example: A Siemens supplier is Infineon. Siemens worked together with Infineon for a long time. Therefore, BenQ can be sure that Infineon will stay a reliable supplier also for BenQ Siemens mobile phones. Infineon agreed completely with the acquisition through BenQ.[44] So, it is almost also a vertical grow. Additionally, European customers think that Asian companies often have minor quality standards. Asian products are seen as low quality products. But BenQ will operate in the high quality

---

[44]http://www.networld.at/index.html?/articles/0523/30/113842.shtml, 07.01.07

segment of IT and consumer electronic.[45] BenQ intended to develop in future a diverse product line, mobile phones with new design. Therefore it is even more crucial to have access to countries companies in order to cooperate with them and let the customers know.

4.2.4 R&D, production facilities

Finally one reason was the takeover of the Research and Development as well as the production facilities in Germany and Manaus. BenQ can use the R&D activities in order to have access to educated staff, knowledge, process innovation, improvement ideas or new technology. Siemens and BenQ announced shortly after the aquisition that both companies have the intention to work closely together. Siemens is known for its high engineering and technological expertise and BenQ for its knowledge about IT and consumer electronic.[46] They would use synergy effects, especially for the distribution, knowledge, know-how and do research together. It could be imagined that BenQ sends employees to the R&D department as well as to production to in order for them to gain knowledge. BenQ could have used Siemens employees to indirectly train BenQ employees. Today after the announcement of the bankruptcy, BenQ can use the knowledge in its related divisions.

4.3 Sum up

It is difficult to give the primum mobile of BenQ why the company acquired the mobile phone division. All reasons and what has been the main motive could only be known BenQ internally. But the four reasons that are provided in that thesis are definitely reasons which influenced the decision makers to build BenQ Siemens. Access to the management is always one of the most important points when going abroad. Despite the bankruptcy, BenQ still can use the acquired knowledge.

5. Conclusion

Finally there is to say that BenQ will overcome the bankruptcy more easily than Siemens. Before BenQ acquired the Siemens mobile phone division, the Taiwanese company was unknown in Germany. At the moment the German population don´t want to buy Siemens BenQ mobile

---

[45]http://winfuture.de/news,20981.html, 07.01.07
[46]http://www.mb.com.ph/issues/2006/04/02/TECH2006040259896.html, 04.01.07

phones because of the angry sentiments regarding the closure, the unemployment of the employees and the shutdown of the last German mobile phone producer. In my opinion, BenQ will now leave the German market for a few years and make its return later.

BenQ is a huge Taiwanese company and it is sure that they will enter the German market over time through another product probably in the low cost segment. At the moment their image is tarnished but people will forget about that over time. If BenQ would buy another German company in a few years, and operate under another brandname, it seems that nobody will care. In February another announcement concerning BenQ and Germany is published. BenQ is one of ten sponsors of the European football cup in 2008.[47] The BenQ chairman warranted the donation of mio. of Euro with its relatedness with Europe. There is different information about the amount of money from 15 to 40 mio. Euro. BenQ´s intention is global publicity for its mobile phones which are now exclusively produced in Asia and Latin America.[48] An IG-Metall representative told that the production facility in Kamp-Lintford is waiting still on over 400 mio. Euro.

In contrary Siemens is a traditional German brand. Siemens is also operating on the German market through a variety of goods other than mobile phones. The German company distributes, for example, many white-goods. The Siemens reputation, especially in Germany will further shrink. Since the announcement in 2005 to sell the mobile phone division, the Siemens reputation went down.[49] The public opinion is that Siemens sold its mobile phone division to BenQ to get rid of the employees. According to many press releases, the public thinks that Siemens knew that there is definitely no chance for the division in future. But if Siemens would be the company under which the mobile phone division went bankrupt. Siemens had to be responsible for the employees what means to pay them compensations. At the moment, Siemens has to battle a big fight. The company is constantly in the news on one hand because of BenQ Siemens, one the other hand because of slush money or even clandestine workers. Siemens has to overcome the bad news and to persuade the public to confidence in the company. Finally, the result will be seen in a few years.

---

[47]http://www.manager-magazin.de/unternehmen/artikel/0,2828,464658,00.html, 12.02.07
[48]http://de.today.reuters.com/news/newsArticle.aspx?type=companiesNews&storyID=2007-02-08T062155Z_01_HUB822903_RTRDEOC_0_DEUTSCHLAND-FIRMEN-BENQ-MOBILE.xml&archived=False, 11.02.07
[49]http://www.business-wissen.de/de/aktuell/kat3/akt35123.html

Bibliography

Contributions from newspapers, journals:

Manager Magazin

07/05 page 22

08/06 page 62

09/06 page 36

10/06 page 26

01/07 page 12

Saarbrücker Zeitung

04/12/06 WIRTSCHAFT Nr 2, Seite A6

04/01/07 WIRTSCHAFT Nr 3, Seite A7

Contributions from the Internet:

Bacoc

http://en.bacoc.com/aboutus/aboutus.htm, 03.02.07

BenQ

http://www.benq.com/page/?pageId=2, 24.11.06
http://www.benq.com/page/?pageId=3, 25.10.06
http://www.benq.com/page/?pageId=5, 12.11.06

http://www.benq.de/press/news.cfm?id=995&cat=0&year=2005, 10.12.06

Bitkom

http://www.bitkom.org/de/presse/43408_41678.aspx, 19.01.07

Business News

http://www.businessnews.com/business/art614,279169.html, 03.01.07

http://www.businessnews.com/business/art614,283628.html, 03.01.07

http://www.businessnews.com/business/art614,273215.html, 03.01.07

http://www.businessnews.com/business/art614,266615.html, 23.12.07

http://www.businessnews.com/business/art614,283628.html?fCMS=e523b5c6c9b9d1e9e11474abc1c95937, 03.01.07

http://www.businessnews.com/business/art614,276873.html, 03.01.07

http://www.business-wissen.de/de/aktuell/kat3/akt35123.html, 12.02.07

Deutsche Welle

http://www.dw-world.de/dw/article/0,2144,2298470,00.html, 03.01.07

http://www.dw-world.de/dw/article/0,2144,2137023,00.html, 10.01.07

Espace

http://www.espace.ch/artikel_311424.html, 11.02.07

Frankfurter Allgemeine

http://www.faz.net/d/invest/meldung.aspx?id=39899560, 10.02.07

http://www.faz.net/d/invest/meldung.aspx?id=39897445, 19.01.2007

Golem

http://www.golem.de/0702/50376.html, 07.02.07

Heise

http://www.heise.de/newsticker/meldung/83269, 06.01.07

http://www.heise.de/newsticker/meldung/83725, 19.01.2007

http://www.heise.de/newsticker/meldung/84675/from/rss09, 02.02.07

Informationszentrum Mobilfunk

http://www.izmf.de/html/de/46461.html, 26.11.06

Inside-Handy.de

http://www.inside-handy.de/news/6959.html, 10.01.07

Manager Magazin

http://www.manager-magazin.de/magazin/artikel/0,2828,bild-691696-427713,00.html, 05.01.07
http://www.manager-magazin.de/it/artikel/0,2828,460342,00.html, 19.01.2007

http://www.manager-magazin.de/unternehmen/artikel/0,2828,464658,00.html, 12.02.07

http://www.manager-magazin.de/unternehmen/artikel/0,2828,464746,00.html, 08.02.07

Networld

http://www.networld.at/index.html?/articles/0523/30/113842.shtml, 07.01.07

n24

http://www.n24.de/wirtschaft_boerse/unternehmen/article.php?articleId=90565, 29.12.06

http://www.n24.de/wirtschaft_boerse/unternehmen/article.php?articleId=88844, 20.12.06

Pressetext

http://www.pressetext.at/pte.mc?pte=060929036, 10.01.07

Reuters Deutschland

http://de.today.reuters.com/news/newsArticle.aspx?type=topNews&storyID=2007-01-
03T142012Z_01_KOE351599_RTRDEOC_0_DEUTSCHLAND-FIRMEN-BENQ-ZF.xml,
03.01.06

http://de.today.reuters.com/news/newsArticle.aspx?type=companiesNews&storyID=2007-02-
08T062155Z_01_HUB822903_RTRDEOC_0_DEUTSCHLAND-FIRMEN-BENQ-MO-
BILE.xml&archived=False, 11.02.07

Sentex

http://www.sentextech.com/about.html, 10.02.07

Siemens

http://www.siemens.com/in-
dex.jsp?sdc_p=ft4mls7uo1244571i1050364pcz2&sdc_bcpath=1327903.s_7,1328954.s_7,105
0364.s_7,&sdc_sid=426724783&, 18.11.06

http://w4.siemens.de/archiv/en/laender.html, 04.12.06
http://w4.siemens.de/archiv/en/beteiligungen/beteiligungen_akt.html, 18.11.06
http://www.siemens.com/Daten/siecom/HQ/CC/Internet/Annual/WORKA-
REA/gb05_ed/templatedata/English/file/binary/E05_00_GB2005_1336469.pdf, 03.01.07

http://www.siemens.com/index.jsp?sdc_p=fmls2uo1032974i1032974pcz3&sdc_bcpath=1327
890.s_2,1032974.s_2,&sdc_sid=430668491&, 18.11.06

http://www.siemens.com/in-
dex.jsp?sdc_p=cfi11000000000015lmo1033036ps2uz3&sdc_bcpath=1327890.s_2%2C10329
74.s_2%2C&sdc_sid=430668491&sdc_m4r=, 18.11.06

http://w4.siemens.de/archiv/en/geschichte/zeitleiste/chronik_2.html, 18.11.06

http://w4.siemens.de/archiv/en/geschichte/zeitleiste/chronik_2.html, 18.11.06

http://w4.siemens.de/archiv/en/dokumente/company_history_long.pdf, 18.11.06

http://w4.siemens.de/archiv/en/dokumente/company_history.pdf, 18.11.06

http://www.siemens.com/in-
dex.jsp?sdc_p=cd1034230fi1273833lmn1031735o1273833ps5uz1&, 05.01.07

Silicon

http://www.silicon.de/enid/wirtschaft_und_politik/25284, 09.02.07

Stern

http://www.stern.de/wirtschaft/unternehmen/unternehmen/:Kommentar-BenQ-
Rei%DFleine/572767.html, 12.12.06

http://www.stern.de/wirtschaft/unternehmen/unternehmen/572777.html?nv=ct_mt, 10.12.06

Spiegelgruppe

http://www.spiegelgruppe.de/spiegel-
gruppe/home.nsf/pmweb/BB855CEFD0E80BB2C12571EF0030AF28, 29.12.06

Spiegel

http://www.spiegel.de/wirtschaft/0,1518,439919,00.html, 03.01.07; 11.11.06

Wallstreet

http://www.wallstreet-online.de/nachrichten/nachricht/1994563.html, 06.01.07

WDR

http://www.wdr.de/themen/wirtschaft/wirtschaftsbran-
che/benq/061229.jhtml?rubrikenstyle=wirtschaft, 02.01.06

http://www.wdr.de/themen/kurzmeldungen/2007/01/01/hiobsbotschaft_fuer_benq-mitarbei-
ter.jhtml?rubrikenstyle=wirtschaft, 01.01.07

Winfuture

http://winfuture.de/news,20981.html, 07.01.07

Wissen

http://www20.wissen.de/wde/generator/wissen/services/nachrichten/ftd/TM/159233.html,
08.02.2007

http://www20.wissen.de/wde/generator/wissen/services/nachrichten/ftd/TM/159233.html,
08.02.07

Yahoo News

http://de.news.yahoo.com/070201/281/5b1ir.html, 02.02.07

Individual Books:

Thomas L. Wheelen, J. David Hunger, Strategic Management and Business Policy, 9th edition,
2004 New Jersey

Lecture notes

Prof. Dr. rer. pol. Mario Glowik, International Market Entry Strategies, 2005, page 8